Alabama

by Anne Welsbacher

Consultant:
Jessica Lacher-Feldman
Public & Outreach Services
Coordinator/Assistant Professor
W.S. Hoole Special Collections Library,
The University of Alabama

Capstone
press
Mankato, Minnesota

Capstone Press
151 Good Counsel Drive • P.O. Box 669 • Mankato, Minnesota 56002
http://www.capstone-press.com

Library of Congress Cataloging-in-Publication Data
Welsbacher, Anne, 1955–
  Alabama / Anne Welsbacher.
  p. cm. —(Land of liberty)
  Summary: Provides an overview of the state of Alabama, covering its
history, geography, government, economy, people, and culture.
  Includes bibliographical references and index.
  ISBN 0-7368-1569-4 (hardcover)
  1. Alabama–Juvenile literature. [1. Alabama.] I. Title. II. Series.
  F326.3 .W45 2003
  976.1–dc21

                                                          2002011694

Editorial Credits
Amanda Doering, editor; Jennifer Schonborn, series designer; Linda Clavel, book designer;
  Angi Gahler, illustrator; Karrey Tweten, photo researcher; Eric Kudalis, product
  planning editor

Photo Credits
Cover images: DeSoto Falls, Corbis/David Muench; Mobile Bay, Index Stock Imagery/Jeff
Greenberg

Alabama Tourism Department, 1, 4, 48; Athens State University/Stephen M. Clark, 50;
Bill Johnson, 56; Bruce Coleman, Inc./Lee Foster, 42; Capstone Press/Gary Sundermeyer, 54;
Capstone Press Archives, 28, 32, 35, 47; Corbis/Chromo Sohm Inc., 24; Corbis/Flip Schulke, 34;
Corbis/Bettmann, 40, 52; Corbis/Douglas Kirkland, 41; Hulton Archive by Getty Images, 30;
Index Stock Imagery/Sherwood Hoffman, 22–23; James P. Rowan, 15, 16–17, 36;
North Wind Picture Archives, 18, 20, 26, 58; One Mile Up, Inc. 55 (both); PhotoDisc, Inc., 57;
Unicorn Stock Photos, 46; U.S. Postal Service, 59; William H. Allen Jr., 8, 10, 12–13, 44–45, 63

Artistic Effects
Creatas, Digital Stock, PhotoDisc, Inc.

1 2 3 4 5 6 08 07 06 05 04 03

Table of Contents

Huge rock formations jut out of the ground and down from the cave ceiling of DeSoto Caverns.

Chapter 1

About Alabama

Mysterious caves lie hidden below the ground in the northeastern part of Alabama. These caves are filled with enormous rock formations. Some of the rocks look like they are dripping from the top of the caves. Other rocks rise out of the cave floor like large spikes. Some areas of these caves are only big enough for one person to squeeze through the rocks. Other areas are huge, open rooms that are 60 feet (18 meters) high.

Cave explorers are called spelunkers. Spelunkers enjoy caves like those in DeSoto Caverns. Spelunkers climb into caves for sport and to search for signs of life. In ancient times, humans lived deep inside the caves. Spelunkers look closely at the rocks for remains of these humans. Some of these explorers are part of a group called the National Speleological Society. The group's home base is in Huntsville.

Visitors explore the caves. They walk through trails and gaze into clear pools of water. Visitors can see some of the country's rarest animals. Many of Alabama's caves are home to the endangered gray bat. Blind cavefish swim in the cave streams. Not only are the fish blind, they do not have eyes at all.

The Heart of Dixie

Alabama has several nicknames. Located in the deep south, the state is known as the Heart of Dixie. Alabama was called the Cradle of the Confederacy during the Civil War. The state is also known as the Cotton State for its cotton production. Tennessee borders Alabama to the north. Mississippi lies to the west, and Georgia to the east. A narrow part of Florida lies south of most of Alabama. Part of Alabama goes south right into the Gulf of Mexico. The state is home to about 4.5 million people.

Alabama Cities

TENNESSEE

MISSISSIPPI

• Florence

• Huntsville

• Decatur

• Gadsden

• Birmingham
Hoover •

• Tuscaloosa

Selma •

⭐ Montgomery

GEORGIA

ALABAMA

Dothan •

Mobile •

FLORIDA

Gulf of Mexico

N
W   E
S

Legend

▪	American Indian Reservation
⭐	Capital
●	City

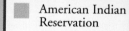

Scale
Miles
0   20   40   60   80

0   20   40   60   80   100
Kilometers

Mobile Bay extends south into the Gulf of Mexico.

8

Chapter 2

Land, Climate, and Wildlife

Alabama is home to many landscapes. The state has mountains, plains, farmlands, wetlands, and beaches. The Appalachian Mountains in the north are the highest part of Alabama. From this point to the south and west, the state drops in height. Mobile Bay at the Gulf of Mexico lies at sea level. This is Alabama's lowest point.

Land Regions

The Gulf Coastal Plain covers two-thirds of Alabama. This large area has several sub-regions. At the southern plain lies the mouth of Mobile Bay. The Wiregrass area is in the southeast.

The Wiregrass area includes a red, sandy area named the Southern Red Hills. The flat, southwestern part of the Gulf Coastal Plain is covered with wetlands.

The Black Belt is part of the Gulf Coastal Plain. The Black Belt cuts through the center of the plain. The rich, black dirt of this land is some of Alabama's best farmland.

The Piedmont Plateau is located in east-central Alabama. Cheaha Mountain, the highest point in the state, is in this area. Cheaha Mountain is 2,407 feet (734 meters) high.

The Appalachian Plateau is also called the Cumberland Plateau. This area is farther north than the Piedmont.

Cheaha Mountain is the highest point in Alabama. This photo shows the scenic view from the top of Cheaha Mountain.

Alabama's Land Features

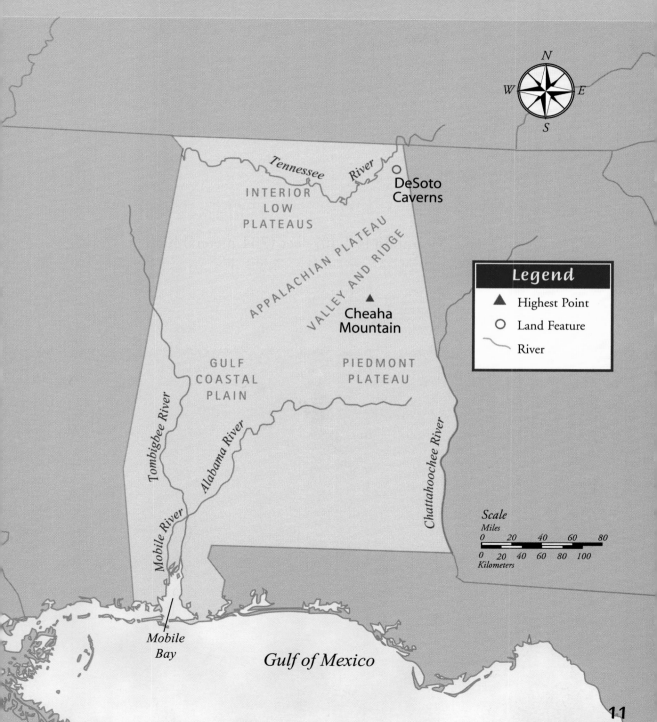

Tennessee River

INTERIOR
LOW
PLATEAUS

DeSoto
Caverns

APPALACHIAN PLATEAU

VALLEY AND RIDGE

Cheaha
Mountain

GULF
COASTAL
PLAIN

PIEDMONT
PLATEAU

Tombigbee River

Alabama River

Mobile River

Chattahoochee River

Mobile
Bay

Gulf of Mexico

Legend

▲ Highest Point

○ Land Feature

～ River

Scale
Miles
0   20   40   60   80

0 20 40 60 80 100
Kilometers

East of the Appalachian Plateau is the Valley and Ridge region. This region is a set of long, narrow valleys between mountain ridges. The Interior Low Plateaus are rolling lands in the northwestern part of the state.

The Water

Alabama's waterways contribute to its economy. Bays in southern Alabama open into the ocean, supporting a thriving port industry. Alabama's rivers carry boats and barges all over

the state. The power of water moving through Alabama's streams and rivers provides electricity.

Alabama has two large river systems. The Tennessee River, in northern Alabama, runs through the Interior Low Plateaus. Dams were built along the Tennessee River system to make lakes. The Mobile-Tensaw is the other river system. This system runs into Mobile Bay to the south.

The state's longest rivers are the Tombigbee and the Alabama. These rivers flow into Mobile Bay.

Barges carry lumber on the Tombigbee River.

"Mobile stays in the heart, loveliest of cities."
–Carl Carmer, travel writer

Climate

Alabama's climate is mild. Summers in the south are hot and humid. Temperatures often reach 100 degrees Fahrenheit (38 degrees Celsius). The state's average summer temperature is about 79 degrees Fahrenheit (26 degrees Celsius). Winters are short and cool. Snow can fall in the winter, but it usually falls only in Alabama's northern hills. The state's average winter temperature is 47 degrees Fahrenheit (8 degrees Celsius).

Forests

Almost two-thirds of Alabama is covered by 22 million acres of forests. More than 125 different kinds of trees are found in the state. These trees include pine, oak, hickory, magnolia, cypress, pecan, and more.

Forests help Alabama's environment, but logging is a major state industry. Forests help keep soil from losing water. Wood from forests is used to build homes and make paper and other products. Alabama's forests support a large paper industry. By the 1950s, Alabama forests had been reduced by heavy logging. In the 1970s, the state began programs to replace forests.

Wildlife

Alabama's birds were once in danger because of overhunting and pollution. Wildlife programs have brought bird populations back to Alabama. Among the birds found in Alabama are great blue herons, brown pelicans, bald eagles, and ospreys. Wild turkeys, cardinals, blue jays, and mockingbirds also live in the state.

Brown pelicans nest along the coastal areas of Alabama.

The state bird is a kind of woodpecker, the brightly colored yellowhammer.

The state's water supports plenty of wildlife. The Cahaba River carries 131 species of fish, more than any other river in the United States. Bass, catfish, crappy, bream, drum fish, and trout swim in Alabama rivers. Flounder, red snapper, oysters, crab, and shrimp live in Mobile Bay. Many sea animals live in the muddy areas where Alabama's rivers meet the Gulf of Mexico. These estuaries are home to alligators, gulf sturgeons, and

snapping turtles. The rare Alabama shovelnose sturgeon also lives there. In 1995, Alabama joined the National Estuary Program. Limits were placed on activities that cause pollution, drain swamps, or hurt these areas.

Even with these programs, some animals and plants are endangered. Endangered birds include the American peregrine falcon and the bald eagle. The rare gray bat that lives in Alabama's caves is in danger. Sea animals such as turtles and the cavefish are also endangered. Some plants are even hard to find. The leafy prairie-clover and the leather flower are rare.

American alligators live in Alabama's estuaries.

Mounds built by ancient people can still be seen in Alabama today.

Chapter 3

History of Alabama

Between 1000 and 1450, mound builders built huge mounds of earth as high as 60 feet (18 meters) tall. Some of these mounds were used as homes for the tribes' leaders. Families buried their dead in other mounds.

Around 1450, the mound builders disappeared. New groups arrived in Alabama. They were members of the Choctaw, Chickasaw, Cherokee, and Creek Indian tribes. One of the Creek tribes was called the Alibamu, meaning "clear the thicket." The state's name of Alabama is based on the tribe's name.

European Settlers and American Indian Conflict

In 1540, Spanish explorer Hernando de Soto arrived in Alabama. He was looking for gold. De Soto took the American Indians' food and horses for his own use. He sometimes killed or enslaved the Indians if they would not tell him where to find gold. Some of the tribes fought back.

Chief Tuscaloosa and his Choctaw people fought de Soto at Maubila village. Tuscaloosa and his people lost this battle, but Spain failed to make the area a colony. More than

Hernando de Soto relied on the American Indians to tell him where to find gold. The reports he heard turned out to be rumors. He never found the gold he was seeking.

150 years passed before any permanent European settlements were made in the area.

Land Wars

In 1702, the French set up Fort Louis de la Mobile near the Mobile River. Great Britain also wanted this land. During the French and Indian War (1754–1763), Great Britain and France fought over land in Alabama and other states. Both countries fought for fur-trading rights in the area. The Treaty of Paris ended the war. In the Treaty of Paris, France gave most of Alabama to Great Britain. Spain still had control over southern Alabama.

In 1783, the American colonies won independence from England in the Revolutionary War (1775–1783). Northern Alabama became part of the United States. Spain still ruled the Gulf Coast area. Both Spain and the United States wanted control over Mobile Bay.

The United States fought battles over this area. The settlers were hostile toward the Creek Indians. The Creek joined British forces to fight the United States in the War of 1812 (1812–1814).

In 1813, Chief Menewa and his Red Stick Creeks attacked U.S. soldiers at Fort Mims near Tensaw, Alabama. Hundreds of soldiers were killed. In 1814, General Andrew Jackson took revenge. He defeated the Red Stick Creeks in the Battle of Horseshoe Bend. The United States finally won the Mobile Bay area from the Spanish.

Several tribes helped Jackson in the Battle of Horseshoe Bend. These tribes included White Stick Creek, Chickasaw, Choctaw, and Cherokee. Even though they helped Jackson,

these tribes were also forced to give up most of their land in Alabama.

In 1817, Alabama became a U.S. territory. In 1819, it became the 22nd state.

Growth and Slavery

Between 1820 and 1830, the population of Alabama doubled. In the 10 years after 1830, the number of people doubled again. Cotton grew on huge farms called plantations.

Land near the Gulf of Mexico was valuable as a shipping port. The United States fought many battles to control this land.

The First White House of the Confederacy still stands in Montgomery.

Southern states often bought slaves from Africa to help with the crops. By 1861, Alabama's slave population almost equaled its white population.

That same year, the Northern and the Southern states went to war. The North wanted the South to free the slaves. The South did not want the North telling them what to do.

Southern states felt that each state should make its own laws.

In 1860, Abraham Lincoln ran for U.S. president with anti-slavery beliefs. When he won, Alabama and six other states left, or seceded from, the United States. Eventually, eleven states seceded. This secession began the Civil War (1861–1865).

Confederacy and the Civil War

The Southern states claimed to be a new country. They called this country the Confederate States of America. They named Jefferson Davis as their president. Montgomery, Alabama, was their capital. For this reason, Alabama became known as the Cradle of the Confederacy. Later, the Confederate capital moved to Richmond, Virginia, because it was closer to the Union capital.

Few Civil War battles were fought in Alabama. Alabama escaped much of the damage that other Southern states experienced. About 122,000 Alabamians fought in the war, and 45,000 Alabamians died in it.

The Battle of Mobile Bay was an important victory for the Union.

One important battle was fought in Mobile Bay. In 1864, the Union tried to take over Mobile Bay. Union Admiral David G. Farragut led the attack. Confederate soldiers sunk one of his ships. Farragut drove his ships into the bay, shouting, "Damn the torpedoes! Full speed ahead!" The Union lost many men, but they won the Battle of Mobile Bay. In 1865, the war ended, and the South was defeated.

Rebellion and Reconstruction

After the Civil War, 500,000 slaves were freed in Alabama. Some Southern whites were angry. Alabama passed Black Codes. These laws said that African Americans could not travel or hold jobs. Alabama also refused to agree to the 14th Amendment to the U.S. Constitution. This amendment gave African Americans the right to vote. Alabama was put under military rule by the federal government until the state passed a new constitution in 1868.

Reconstruction efforts from 1868 to 1874 were meant to help the South rebuild. During this time, Southern states were run by Northern leaders. These leaders were often dishonest.

Freed slaves farmed land on plantations to make a living. They gave part of their crops to the land owners to pay for supplies. Land owners charged so much for food and supplies that African Americans stayed in debt. This system, called sharecropping, was not much better than slavery for African Americans.

In 1874, the Northerners left. Alabama passed a new state constitution taking away many rights for African Americans. In 1896, the U.S. Supreme Court allowed the forced separation of whites and African Americans. This practice was called segregation. A 1901 Alabama constitution limited African American voting rights. These limits were kept in place for 50 years.

Industrial Growth

Before the Civil War, Alabamians still grew cotton, but began mining iron and coal. As railroads and other industries grew, Birmingham became a center for iron and steel in the south.

Cotton was Alabama's most important crop in the early 1900s.

Still, cotton farming remained Alabama's largest industry. In 1913, a small bug called the boll weevil destroyed most of the cotton crop. Alabamians were forced to plant peanuts and other kinds of crops. Planting different crops proved to be better for the land. It also helped Alabama develop a stronger economy.

The 1920s and 1930s brought many ups and downs to Alabama. World War I (1914–1918) increased the country's need for food, cotton, steel, and textiles. These industries brought money into the state. But the Great Depression (1929–1939) hurt the entire country, including Alabama. Many people lost their jobs and their land. Floods and hurricanes also struck Alabama in the 1930s. The New Deal, developed by President Franklin D. Roosevelt, made many programs to help Americans. In Alabama, the Tennessee Valley Authority (TVA) used Alabama's rivers to provide cheap electricity.

Tuskegee Airmen

In 1941, the government created the first African American military pilot program. These soldiers were trained to fly at the Tuskegee Institute in Alabama. The pilots were called the Tuskegee Airmen. Many of the first airmen flew with the famous 99th Fighter Squadron in World War II. The Tuskegee Airmen shot down more than 1,000 German planes during the war. Even though African American and white pilots were separated, the Tuskegee Airmen fought many battles with white squadrons.

World War II (1939–1945) brought money to Alabama again as its factories made war supplies. The warm climate made Alabama a good place for military training camps. Many sharecroppers moved off farms and into factories to make war supplies. After World War II, Alabama relied less on farming.

Alabama became a key player in early space exploration. The first U.S. satellite sent into space was developed at a military base in Huntsville. In 1958, the satellite *Explorer I* was sent into space. NASA's Marshall Space Flight Center was built in Huntsville in 1960.

Civil Rights Movement

Even in the 1950s, African Americans were not treated fairly in work, housing, education, and other areas. Since 1901, Alabama's laws had limited African American voting rights. African Americans were still segregated from whites. They went to separate schools and had to sit at the backs of public buses. They could not use the same restrooms as whites or eat in the same restaurants.

In the 1950s, African Americans worked to change their lives. In 1955, Rosa Parks refused to give her seat in the front of a bus to a white man in Montgomery. She was arrested. A Baptist minister, Dr. Martin Luther King Jr., asked African

Americans in Montgomery to refuse to use the buses. This movement was called the Montgomery Bus Boycott. The boycott lasted more than a year. Without the African American customers, the bus company lost money. The boycott also drew national attention to the African American cause. The bus boycott was the first of many nonviolent actions taken by African Americans to gain their rights. These actions were part of the the Civil Rights Movement.

Rosa Parks was arrested in Montgomery for refusing to give up her seat on a bus to a white man.

In 1954, the U.S. Supreme Court ordered schools to let all races attend school together. This process of integration was not easy. In 1963, Governor George Wallace stood in front of the University of Alabama. He tried to keep two African American students from registering for classes at the school. The National Guard was sent to force Wallace to let them attend the school.

In 1963, many violent acts took place in Alabama. Peaceful protesters were hurt by city officials and police dogs. In Birmingham, four African American girls died when their church was bombed.

In 1964, the U.S. government passed the Civil Rights Act. This act was created to make sure people of all races were treated equally. Many states did not follow the new laws. As a result, most African Americans in Alabama still could not vote. In 1965, Dr. Martin Luther King Jr. led hundreds of people in a march from Selma to Montgomery. Peaceful marchers were beaten and teargassed by police and citizens.

TV cameras recorded the scenes. Two weeks later, more than 3,000 people came from all over the United States to join the march. National Guard troops protected the marchers. In August, the U.S. government passed the Voting Rights Act of 1965. The act gave equal voting rights to all people.

Alabama Today

Since the late 1900s, race issues have improved. A Civil Rights Memorial was built in 1989. The memorial reminds people of the struggle that African Americans went through to gain

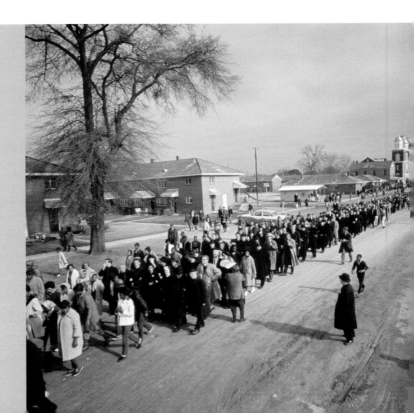

In 1965, thousands of people marched from Selma to Montgomery to protest unfair voting rights.

Dr. Martin Luther King Jr.

Dr. Martin Luther King Jr. was one of the most powerful Civil Rights leaders in history. King wanted equal rights for African Americans, but he did not want to use violence. King set up peaceful protests and marches. These peaceful actions made the country aware of the conditions of African Americans.

King was also a pastor. He preached at the Dexter Street Baptist Church in Montgomery. King's wife, Corretta Scott King, was from Alabama.

their rights. More African American Alabamians were elected into public office. In 2001, African American Condoleezza Rice from Alabama was chosen as the National Security Advisor. She is the first woman to hold this position.

Alabama is poorer than the average U.S. state, but Alabama is working to improve its economy. It has moved away from farming and into other industries. These industries include textiles, paper, and manufacturing. The need for workers has helped Alabama's population grow.

The capitol building stands in Montgomery. The original capitol building was built in 1847, but burned down in 1849. The new capitol was finished in 1851.

Government and Politics

Alabama's constitution is longer than any other state's. It has been changed more than 700 times. Like many southern states, Alabama is conservative in politics. Alabama has voted Republican in presidential elections since 1980.

Branches of Government

Alabama's government has an executive, legislative, and judicial branch. The executive branch carries out the laws. This branch includes the governor and lieutenant governor. These two positions are elected separately. The governor and lieutenant governor may belong to different political parties.

"Our state government is for all. So let us join together, for Alabama belongs to all of us—black and white, young and old, rich and poor alike."

—George Wallace, former Alabama governor

Both positions are elected every four years. Governors are limited to serving two terms in a row.

At one point, Alabama's governor was limited to serving one term. Governor George Wallace served one term, from 1963–1967. After his term, his wife, Lurleen, ran and was elected. Wallace returned as governor in 1971. By this time, the constitution had been changed. He was able to serve two more terms in a row. Wallace served a fourth term beginning in 1983.

Alabama's legislative branch includes a 35-member senate and a 105-member house. Members serve four-year terms. Legislators write new laws and vote to pass them. Laws then go to the governor to sign or reject. If the bill is rejected, lawmakers can turn the bill into a new law if enough members agree.

The judicial branch interprets the laws and tries court cases. The Alabama judicial branch includes the supreme court, the appellate courts, and the court of the judiciary. Nine judges make up the supreme court. Each judge serves six-year terms. The civil appeals court and the criminal appeals court make up the appellate courts. Each appeals court has six judges.

Alabama's State Government

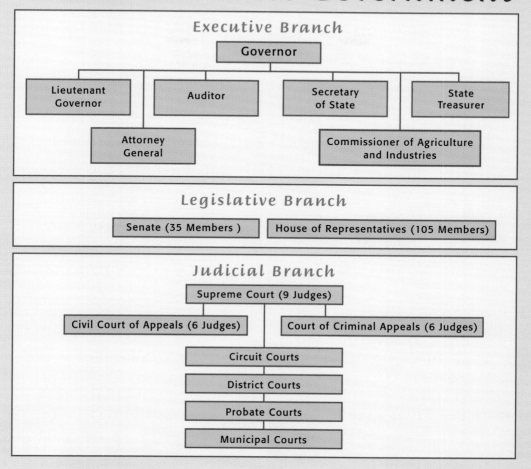

Executive Branch

Governor

Lieutenant Governor | Auditor | Secretary of State | State Treasurer

Attorney General | Commissioner of Agriculture and Industries

Legislative Branch

Senate (35 Members) | House of Representatives (105 Members)

Judicial Branch

Supreme Court (9 Judges)

Civil Court of Appeals (6 Judges) | Court of Criminal Appeals (6 Judges)

Circuit Courts

District Courts

Probate Courts

Municipal Courts

Scottsboro Boys Trial

U.S. court systems are set up to decide the guilt or innocence of people accused of a crime. The systems try to be fair. Alabama is known for a case in the 1930s in which African Americans were not tried fairly. This case was called the

Scottsboro Boys trial. In this case, nine African American men were accused of attacking two white women.

Evidence did not show the men were guilty. But an all-white jury found the men guilty. They were sentenced to die. The case went to the U.S. Supreme Court. This court found they had not been fairly tried. The men had another trial. They were again found guilty, even though one of the women said the attack never happened. A third trial also said the men were guilty, but was rejected by the U.S. Supreme Court.

The Scottsboro Boys were tried three times for attacking two white women. They were finally judged innocent and set free.

George Wallace

George Wallace first ran for governor in 1958. He wanted more rights for African Americans and other poor Alabamians. But Wallace lost, and he changed his image. He was elected governor of Alabama in 1962. In 1963, he drew attention to Alabama. Wallace refused to allow black students to enter the University of Alabama. In 1968 and again in 1972, he ran for U.S. president. During his 1972 campaign, he was shot. He survived, but he could not move his legs, so he used a wheelchair. Wallace's views on race changed again. He supported equal rights for all races. In 1982, he won a large percentage of the African American vote in Alabama. It was his fourth election for governor of Alabama. Wallace died in 1998.

In 1937, the four youngest men were released from jail. The last man in the Scottsboro case spent 19 years in jail before being judged innocent and set free.

Peanuts grow underneath the ground. Alabama is the third largest producer of peanuts in the nation.

Chapter 5

Economy and Resources

Cotton was king in Alabama during its early years as a state. The warm climate, good rainfall, and rich soil supported plantations. In the early 1900s, farmers grew peanuts and soybeans instead of just cotton. They also raised poultry, cattle, and hogs. They sold eggs and other products. These products now make up about two-thirds of Alabama's farming income. Today, Alabama is the third-largest peanut producer in the United States.

Agriculture is no longer a major industry in Alabama. About four percent of the state's income is from farming.

Alabama's Industries

More than 25 percent of Alabamians work in manufacturing and construction. They make paper, auto parts, chemicals, textiles, metals, machinery, and rubber. Three large automobile plants make auto parts in Alabama.

Lumber and forest products are the number one manufacturing industry in Alabama. About 68 percent of Alabama is forested. Mostly pine is harvested. Oak, gum, and yellow poplar trees are also sold for wood, paper, and for other products.

In the mid-1800s, Alabama began mining coal, iron, and other minerals. Alabama is eighth in the United States in coal production. Most of the coal is in northern Alabama. Oil and natural gas are drilled in the southern part of the state. While still important today, mining makes up only 2 percent of the state's industry.

The rivers and ports of Alabama support a healthy transportation industry. River barges move through the Tennessee-Tombigbee Waterway from southern Alabama to

Oil rigs drill for oil in Mobile Bay.

the Gulf of Mexico. Mobile is home to one of the country's most important shipping ports.

Service industries are the largest industry in Alabama today. Almost 70 percent of Alabamians work in service industries. Trade is the leading service industry. Community services, finance, and insurance are also important.

Tourism is another important service industry in Alabama. The U.S. Space and Rocket Center in Huntsville is a popular tourist spot. Students of all ages can go to Space Camp and learn about becoming an astronaut. People also come to enjoy the natural beauty of the state's parks, rivers, and beaches.

Kids can go to Space Camp at the U.S. Space and Rocket Center in Huntsville.

George Washington Carver

George Washington Carver was one of the country's most well-known agricultural scientists. At the Tuskegee Institute, Carver found that cotton took certain minerals from the soil. Over time, this made it impossible to grow anything in the soil. He found that peanuts, soybeans, and sweet potatoes used up minerals too, but added other minerals to the soil.

Many Alabamians are employed in the technology industry. The Marshall Space Flight Center in Huntsville explores space-related projects. New technologies being studied there include rocket engine systems that use oxygen from the air. Scientists are also exploring how rockets can use the sun's energy.

Medical technology is also a growing industry in Alabama. The Southern Research Institute in Birmingham studies diseases. It is one of the top six institutions in the country in cancer and AIDS research.

People make colorful floats for the Mardi Gras parade and festival.

Chapter 6

People and Culture

About three out of five Alabamians live in cities. The largest cities are Birmingham, Mobile, Montgomery, and Huntsville. These cities are home to large populations of African Americans and Hispanic Americans.

Alabama is home to about 22,400 American Indians. About 200 of these Indians live on the Poarch Creek Reservation in southern Alabama.

The Arts in Alabama

Alabamians like to celebrate the arts and culture. The oldest Mardi Gras Festival is held in Mobile. The festival has been celebrated there since the early 1700s. The annual Birmingham International Festival celebrates a new country and culture each year. Montgomery's Shakespeare Festival supports theatre, music, and dance programs. The Montgomery festival is the fifth-largest Shakespeare festival in the world.

Alabamians enjoy the arts, especially traditional American music. They listen to country western, blues, gospel, folk, and jazz music. Fiddles, banjos, guitars, and mandolins are among the popular folk instruments in Alabama. The W.C. Handy Music Festival in Florence is named for the father of the blues.

Alabamians enjoy playing and listening to folk music. These young musicians are playing at the W.C. Handy Music Festival.

Alabama's Ethnic Backgrounds

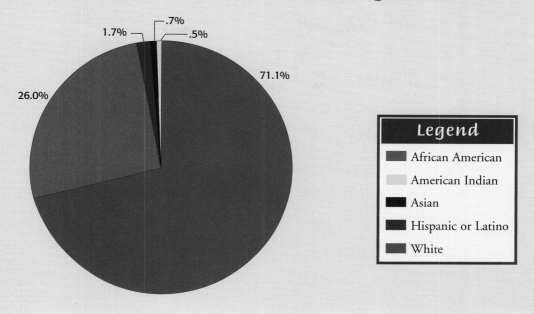

.7%

1.7%

.5%

71.1%

26.0%

Legend

African American

American Indian

Asian

Hispanic or Latino

White

The Tennessee Valley Old Time Fiddlers Convention is held in Athens, Alabama. The convention draws people from all over the south. These people compete for prizes in musical instrument contests. They also compete in old-time singing and dancing contests.

Folk art also is an Alabama tradition. Art fairs feature quilts, pottery, and dolls made by Alabama artists. Alabama's Kentuck Festival of the Arts is celebrated in Northport. The festival features the work of more than 300 artists, including many Alabamians.

Alabama Literature

Alabama has been home to many famous authors and classic works of literature. *To Kill a Mockingbird* was written by Alabamian writer Harper Lee. The book won a Pulitzer prize. It was made into a movie that won an Academy Award. The story is similar to the real Alabama trial of the Scottsboro Boys. Other Alabamian authors include Zelda Fitzgerald, Mary Ward Brown, and William March.

Much like Alabama's scenery, the people of Alabama are varied and unique. The Heart of Dixie has been the birthplace

In the movie, *To Kill a Mockingbird*, a single father raises his two children while trying to defend an innocent African American man.

Helen Keller

Helen Keller was a writer and speaker who worked to help people like herself. Keller was born in Tuscumbia, Alabama. She became blind and deaf after a childhood sickness. Her teacher, Anne Sullivan, taught Keller how to read and write. Keller went to Radcliffe College and became the first deaf and blind person to earn a college degree. Keller and Sullivan traveled all over the world speaking to people. Keller wrote several books. Plays and movies have featured her struggles to overcome her disabilities.

of many influential people and events. Alabamians have proven their motto, "We dare defend our rights." In the face of change and challenge, Alabamians stand tall and proud.

Recipe: Peanut Butter Pie

Peanuts are an important crop in Alabama. Alabama is the third largest producer of peanuts in the United States.

Ingredients

1 4-ounce (110-gram) package
    cream cheese, softened
½ cup (120 mL) powdered
    sugar
1 cup (240 mL) peanut butter
½ cup (120 mL) milk
8-ounce (225-gram) tub
    whipped topping
1 chocolate pie crust

To Serve
8 ounces (225 grams) whipped
    topping
¼ cup (60 mL) chocolate syrup

Equipment

medium mixing bowl
electric mixer
dry ingredient measuring cup
liquid measuring cup
mixing spoons

What You Do

1. Leave the cream cheese out for several hours to soften.

2. In a mixing bowl, mix the cream cheese and sugar with electric mixer until creamy.

3. Add the peanut butter and milk to the mixture.

4. Beat slowly for 3 minutes until smooth.

5. Add 8 ounces (225 grams) whipped topping to the mixture.

6. With a mixing spoon, blend in the whipped topping until no streaks of white are left.

7. Unwrap the chocolate pie crust.

8. Pour mixture into the pie crust.

9. Freeze in freezer for at least 2 hours.

To Serve
1. Spread whipped topping on pie.

2. Drizzle chocolate syrup on top of whipped topping.

Makes 6 servings

Alabama's Flag and Seal

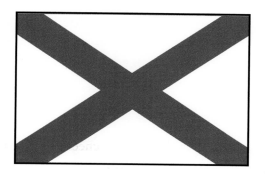

Alabama's Flag

The Alabama state flag shows a crimson St. Andrew's cross on a white background. The flag was patterned after the Confederate Battle Flag, and was adopted in 1895.

Alabama's Seal

The state seal shows a map of Alabama and features its many rivers. It was designed by Alabama's first governor, William Wyatt Bibb. The seal was adopted in 1819 but was only used until 1869. Then a new seal was adopted for Reconstruction. The original great seal was adopted again in 1939.

Almanac

General Facts

Nicknames: Heart of Dixie, Cotton State

Population: 4,447,100 (U.S. Census 2000)
Population rank: 23rd

Capital: Montgomery

Largest cities:
Birmingham, Montgomery, Mobile, Huntsville, Hoover

Agriculture

Agricultural products:
Chickens, beef, eggs, hogs, cotton, peanuts, soybeans

Climate

Average winter temperature:
47 degrees Fahrenheit (8 degrees Celsius)

Average summer temperature:
79 degrees Fahrenheit (26 degrees Celsius)

Annual precipitation:
52 inches (127 centimeters)

Geography

Area: 52,237 square miles (135,294 square kilometers)
Size rank: 30th

Highest elevation: Cheaha Mountain, 2,407 feet (734 meters) above sea level

Lowest elevation: Mobile Bay, sea level

Camilla

Economy

Major industries: Wholesale and retail trade services, manufacturing

Natural resources: Stone, lumber, lime, coal

Government

First governor: William Wyatt Bibb

Statehood: December 24, 1819; 22nd state

U.S. Representatives: 7

U.S. Senators: 2

Electoral votes: 9

Counties: 67

Symbols

Bird: Yellowhammer

Flower: Camilla

Reptile: Red-bellied turtle

Symbols

Tree: Southern longleaf pine

Motto: We dare defend our rights

Song: "Alabama," written by Julia S. Tutwiler, composed by Edna Gockel Gussen

Cotton plant

Timeline

State History

1540
Hernando de Soto arrives and battles the Choctaw Indians.

1702
French settlers set up Fort Louis in Mobile.

1783
Most of Alabama becomes U.S. land.

1814
The Battle of Horseshoe Bend led by Andrew Jackson ends in defeat for the Creek Indians.

1819
Alabama becomes the 22nd state.

1861
Alabama is the fourth state to secede from the United States. Montgomery becomes the first capital of the Confederacy.

1868
Alabama is re-admitted to th United States aft ratifying the 14t amendment.

U.S. History

1620
Pilgrims arrive in New England.

1775–1783
Great Britain and the United States fight the Revolutionary War.

1861–1865
The North and the South fight the Civil War.

1868–1874
Reconstruction efforts are made rebuild the South

3
boll weevil
oys most of
ama's cotton crop.

1931
Scottsboro Boys
trial begins.

1955
Rosa Parks is
arrested. The
Montgomery Bus
Boycott begins.

1965
Dr. Martin Luther
King Jr. leads protesters
on a march from Selma
to Montgomery. The
Voting Rights Act of
1965 is passed.

1963
African American
students attend the
University of
Alabama for the
first time.

1989
A Civil Rights
memorial is built
in Montgomery.

1929–1939
The United States
experiences the
Great Depression.

1964
The Civil Rights Act
is passed, making
discrimination illegal.

1914–1918
World War I is
fought. The
United states
enters the war
in 1917.

1939–1945
World War II
is fought. The
United States enters
the war in 1941.

2001
Terrorists attack
the World Trade
Center and the
Pentagon on
September 11.

Words to Know

boll weevil (BOHL WEE-vil)—a beetle that eats cotton plants

Civil Rights movement—the actions by thousands of people in the mid-1900s to gain equal rights for all people

confederacy (kuhn-FED-ur-uh-see)—the 11 Southern states that withdrew from the United States

integration (in-tuh-GRAY-shuhn)—the mixing of different races

plantation (plan-TAY-shuhn)—a large farm with workers, usually slaves, that live on the land and farm it

Reconstruction (ree-kuhn-STRUHKT-shuhn)—the period of time, from about 1868 to 1874, when the U.S. government tried to rebuild Southern states as they rejoined the United States following the Civil War

secede (si-SEED)—to withdraw; the Confederate states seceded from the Union.

segregation (seg-ruh-GAY-shuhn)—the forced separation of races

sharecropper (SHAIR-crah-pur)—a person who farms a piece of land and pays the owner of the land with money from the crops raised

spelunker (spi-LUHGN-ker)—a person who explores caves

To Learn More

Feeney, Kathy. *Alabama.* From Sea to Shining Sea. New York: Children's Press, 2002.

Koestler, Rachel A. *Going to School During the Civil Rights Movement.* Going to School in History. Mankato, Minn.: Blue Earth Books, 2002.

Martin, Michael A. *Alabama: The Heart of Dixie.* Milwaukee, Wis.: World Almanac, 2002.

Peacock, Judith. *Reconstruction: Rebuilding After the Civil War.* Mankato, Minn.: Bridgestone Books, 2003.

Internet Sites

Track down many sites about Alabama.
Visit the FACT HOUND at *http://www.facthound.com*

IT IS EASY! IT IS FUN!
1) Go to *http://www.facthound.com*
2) Type in: 0736815694
3) Click on "FETCH IT" and FACT HOUND will find several links hand-picked by our editors.

Relax and let our pal FACT HOUND do the research for you!

Places to Write and Visit

Alabama Department of Archives & History
624 Washington Avenue
Montgomery, AL 36130-0100

Alabama State Council on the Arts
& the Alabama Artists Gallery
201 Monroe Street
Montgomery, AL 36130-1800

Alabama Tourism and Travel
P.O. Box 4927
401 Adams Avenue
Montgomery, AL 36103

Civil Rights Memorial
Southern Poverty Law Center
400 Washington Avenue
Montgomery, AL 36101-0548

Office of the Secretary of State
P.O. Box 5616
Montgomery, AL 36130

U.S. Space and Rocket Center
One Tranquility Base
Huntsville, AL 35805

Cypress trees grow in
Alabama's wetlands.

Index

T 57129